Table of Contents

Double-Coated Chicken 4

Kellogg's Corn Flakes® Cookies 6

Cheddar Meatballs 8

Frosted Lemon Bars 10

Kellogg's Corn Flakes® Banana Bread 12

Salmon Burgers with Basil Mayonnaise 14

Crispy French Toast 16

Holiday Mashed Potatoes 18

Kellogg's Corn Flakes® Jumbles 20

Corn-Crab Cakes with Chipotle Sauce 22

Caramel Chews 24

Creamy Broccoli-Cauliflower Casserole 26

Creamy Green Bean Casserole 28

Cherry Bars 30

Double-Coated Chicken

PREP TIME: 30 minutes ■ TOTAL TIME: 1 hour 30 minutes

Makes 8 servings

- **7 cups *Kellogg's Corn Flakes*® Cereal, crushed to 1¾ cups, or 1¾ cups *Kellogg's*® Corn Flake Crumbs**
- **1 egg**
- **1 cup fat-free milk**
- **1 cup all-purpose flour**
- **½ teaspoon salt**
- **¼ teaspoon pepper**
- **3 pounds chicken pieces (without or with skin), rinsed and dried**
- **3 tablespoons margarine or butter, melted**

1. Place KELLOGG'S CORN FLAKES cereal in shallow dish or pan. Set aside.

2. In medium mixing bowl, beat egg and milk slightly. Add flour, salt and pepper. Mix until smooth. Dip chicken in batter. Coat with cereal. Place in single layer, in shallow baking pan coated with cooking spray or foil lined. Drizzle with margarine.

3. Bake at 350°F about 1 hour or until chicken is tender, no longer pink and juices run clear. Do not cover pan or turn chicken while baking. Serve hot.

Corn Flakes® Cookies

PREP TIME: 30 minutes ■ **TOTAL TIME: 1 hour**

Makes 30 cookies

- **2 cups all-purpose flour**
- **½ teaspoon salt**
- **1 cup butter or margarine, softened**
- **⅔ cup sugar**
- **3 egg yolks**
- **½ teaspoon grated lemon peel**
- **1 teaspoon vanilla extract**
- **2 cups *Kellogg's Corn Flakes*® Cereal, crushed to ½ cup**

1. Stir together flour and salt. Set aside.

2. In large mixing bowl, beat together butter, sugar, egg yolks, lemon peel and vanilla until well combined. Add flour mixture, mixing well. Portion and shape dough into 1-inch balls. Roll in KELLOGG'S CORN FLAKES cereal. Place on ungreased baking sheets, about 2 inches apart. Flatten slightly.

3. Bake at 375°F about 8 minutes or until edges are lightly browned. Remove from baking sheets and cool on wire racks. Store in airtight container.

Cheddar Meatballs

PREP TIME: 20 minutes ■ TOTAL TIME: 35 minutes

Makes 3 dozen meatballs

2½ cups *Kellogg's Corn Flakes®* Cereal, divided
2 eggs
⅓ cup milk
½ teaspoon salt
⅛ teaspoon pepper
⅛ teaspoon nutmeg
½ pound ground beef
1 cup shredded Cheddar cheese (4 ounces)

1. Measure 2 cups of the KELLOGG'S CORN FLAKES cereal into medium mixing bowl. Crush slightly. Add eggs and milk. Mix well. Let stand 5 minutes or until cereal softens. Stir in salt, pepper and nutmeg. Add beef and cheese, mixing until combined.

2. Crush the remaining 1½ cups cereal into fine crumbs. Shape beef mixture into 1-inch meatballs. Roll in cereal crumbs. Place in single layer in shallow baking pan coated with cooking spray.

3. Bake at 400°F about 12 minutes or until browned. Serve as appetizer with chili sauce dip or as entrée with buttered noodles. Serve hot.

Frosted Lemon Bars

PREP TIME: 30 minutes ■ TOTAL TIME: 50 minutes

Makes 36 bars

- **2 cups *Kellogg's Corn Flakes*® Cereal, crushed to ½ cup, or ½ cup *Kellogg's*® Corn Flake Crumbs**
- **1 cup all-purpose flour**
- **⅓ cup firmly packed brown sugar**
- **⅓ cup margarine or butter, softened**
- **2 tablespoons all-purpose flour**
- **¼ teaspoon salt**
- **2 eggs, slightly beaten**
- **1 cup firmly packed brown sugar**
- **1½ cups flaked coconut**
- **½ teaspoon vanilla extract**
- **1 cup chopped nuts**
- **1 cup powdered sugar**
- **1 tablespoon margarine, melted**
- **1 tablespoon lemon juice**

1. In large mixing bowl, combine KELLOGG'S CORN FLAKES cereal, 1 cup flour, ⅓ cup brown sugar and margarine. Mix well. Press evenly in bottom of 13×9×2-inch baking pan.

2. Bake at 275°F for 10 minutes. Remove baked crust from oven. Set aside. Increase oven temperature to 350°F.

3. Mix together 2 tablespoons flour and salt. Set aside.

4. In medium mixing bowl, combine eggs, 1 cup brown sugar, coconut and vanilla. Add flour mixture and nuts. Mix well. Spread over baked crust.

5. Return to oven and bake 20 minutes or until bars are lightly browned.

6. While bars are baking, make Lemon Icing. Combine powdered sugar, 1 tablespoon margarine and lemon juice. Beat until smooth. After bars are baked and still warm, frost with Lemon Icing. Cool and cut into bars.

Kellogg's Corn Flakes® Banana Bread

PREP TIME: 20 minutes ■ **TOTAL TIME: 1 hour**

Makes 1 loaf (16 slices per loaf)

- **2 cups all-purpose flour**
- **1 teaspoon baking powder**
- **½ teaspoon baking soda**
- **½ teaspoon salt**
- **1½ cups mashed, ripe bananas**
- **2½ cups *Kellogg's Corn Flakes®* Cereal**
- **½ cup margarine or butter, softened**
- **¾ cup sugar**
- **2 eggs**
- **½ cup coarsely chopped walnuts**

1. Stir together flour, baking powder, baking soda and salt. Set aside.

2. In medium mixing bowl, combine bananas and KELLOGG'S CORN FLAKES cereal. Let stand 5 minutes or until cereal softens. Beat well.

3. In large mixing bowl, beat margarine and sugar until combined. Add eggs. Beat well. Mix in cereal mixture and nuts. Stir in flour mixture. Spread batter evenly in 9×5×3-inch loaf pan coated with cooking spray.

4. Bake at 350°F about 1 hour or until wooden pick inserted near center comes out clean. Let cool 10 minutes before removing from pan. Cool completely before slicing. Wrap with plastic wrap.

Salmon Burgers with Basil Mayonnaise

PREP TIME: 20 minutes ■ TOTAL TIME: 30 minutes

Makes 4 servings

- **2 tablespoons reduced-fat mayonnaise**
- **⅓ cup chopped fresh basil, divided**
- **1 tablespoon reduced-fat sour cream**
- **½ teaspoon grated lemon peel**
- **1 egg, slightly beaten**
- **½ cup *Kellogg's®* Corn Flake Crumbs or 1 cup *Kellogg's Corn Flakes®* Cereal, crushed to ½ cup**
- **¼ cup reduced-fat sour cream**
- **2 tablespoons lemon juice**
- **2 tablespoons finely chopped red onions**
- **1 can (14¾ ounces) salmon, drained, flaked and skin and bones removed**

1. In small bowl, stir together mayonnaise, 2 tablespoons of the basil, 1 tablespoon sour cream and lemon peel. Cover and refrigerate until serving time.

2. Lightly coat cold grill rack with cooking spray. In medium bowl, stir together remaining basil, egg, KELLOGG'S CORN FLAKE crumbs, ¼ cup sour cream, lemon juice and onions. Add salmon; mix well. Shape into four ½-inch-thick patties.

3. Grill over medium heat for 10 minutes or until lightly browned, turning once. Serve topped with mayonnaise mixture.

NOTE: Patties may also be cooked in contact grill. Preheat contact grill for 5 minutes. Cook patties in grill about 5 minutes or until lightly browned. Serve as directed above.

Crispy French Toast

PREP TIME: 10 minutes ■ **TOTAL TIME: 10 minutes**

Makes 4 servings

2 cups *Kellogg's®* Corn Flake Crumbs or 8 cups *Kellogg's Corn Flakes®* Cereal, crushed to 2 cups
2 cups milk
2 eggs
½ cup sugar
1 tablespoon cinnamon
8 slices stale bread
Maple syrup (optional)

1. Place KELLOGG'S CORN FLAKE crumbs in shallow pan. Set aside.

2. In medium bowl, combine milk, eggs, sugar and cinnamon. Dip bread into egg mixture coating both sides of bread. Coat bread with KELLOGG'S CORN FLAKE crumbs.

3. On grill or in large fry pan coated with cooking spray, cook bread on medium heat until both sides are golden brown, turning once. Serve hot with warm maple syrup.

Holiday Mashed Potatoes

PREP TIME: 40 minutes ■ TOTAL TIME: 3 hours 20 minutes

Makes 10 servings

8 medium potatoes (about 3 pounds)
6 sun-dried tomatoes (not packed in oil)
¾ cup sour cream
4 ounces cream cheese, softened and cut into pieces
3 tablespoons butter or margarine, divided
1 clove garlic, minced
¾ teaspoon salt
¼ teaspoon pepper
2 tablespoons to ¼ cup milk
½ cup sliced green onions
⅓ cup *Kellogg's*® Corn Flake Crumbs
2 tablespoons finely shredded Parmesan cheese
2 tablespoons chopped fresh parsley

1. Peel and quarter potatoes. In Dutch oven, cook potatoes in enough boiling salted water to cover for 20 to 25 minutes or until tender.

2. Meanwhile, in small bowl, combine tomatoes and enough hot water to cover. Let stand for 10 minutes. Drain. Finely chop. Set aside.

3. Mash potatoes with potato masher (or in large mixing bowl, beat on low speed of electric mixer until mashed). Add sour cream, cream cheese, 2 tablespoons of the butter, garlic, salt and pepper. Mix until well combined. Gradually mix in enough milk to make potatoes light and fluffy. Fold in onions and tomatoes.

4. Spoon into 2-quart casserole coated with cooking spray. Cover and refrigerate for 2 to 48 hours. Bake, uncovered, at 350°F for 40 minutes.

5. Meanwhile, melt remaining butter. In small bowl, toss together KELLOGG'S CORN FLAKE crumbs, Parmesan cheese, parsley and butter. Uncover potatoes. Sprinkle with crumbs mixture. Bake, uncovered at 350°F for 15 minutes or until top is browned and potatoes are heated through.

NOTE: Casserole may also be reheated in microwave oven. Prepare potatoes as above. Microwave, covered, at high for 9 minutes or until hot, turning and stirring twice. Uncover. Sprinkle with crumbs mixture. Microwave, uncovered, at high for 1 minute more.

Kellogg's Corn Flakes® Jumbles

PREP TIME: 30 minutes ■ TOTAL TIME: 1 hour 15 minutes

Makes 32 cookies

- **1 cup all-purpose flour**
- **½ teaspoon baking powder**
- **¼ teaspoon baking soda**
- **½ teaspoon salt**
- **⅓ cup margarine or butter, softened**
- **½ cup sugar**
- **1 egg, well beaten**
- **½ teaspoon vanilla extract**
- **1½ tablespoons milk**
- **½ cup chopped walnuts**
- **½ cup finely chopped dates**
- **2 cups *Kellogg's Corn Flakes*® Cereal, crushed to ½ cup**

1. Stir together flour, baking powder, baking soda and salt. Set aside.

2. In medium mixing bowl, beat margarine and sugar until thoroughly combined. Add egg, vanilla and milk. Beat well. Add flour mixture, mixing until combined. Stir in walnuts and dates.

3. Place KELLOGG'S CORN FLAKES cereal in shallow dish or pan. Roll teaspoonfuls of dough in cereal. Place on baking sheet coated with cooking spray. Flatten slightly.

4. Bake at 375°F about 12 minutes or until golden brown. Cool completely on wire racks. Store in airtight container.

Corn-Crab Cakes with Chipotle Sauce

PREP TIME: 10 minutes ■ **TOTAL TIME: 15 minutes**

Makes 2 servings

3 tablespoons mayonnaise
¾ teaspoon chipotle hot pepper sauce, divided
1 egg, slightly beaten
⅓ cup *Kellogg's*® Corn Flake Crumbs, divided
¼ cup fresh or frozen corn
2 tablespoons sliced green onions
1 teaspoon Dijon mustard
½ teaspoon coriander
1 can (6 ounces) crabmeat, drained, flaked and cartilage removed
2 teaspoons butter or margarine

1. In small bowl, stir together mayonnaise and ½ teaspoon pepper sauce. Cover and refrigerate until serving time.

2. In medium bowl, stir together egg, ¼ cup KELLOGG'S CORN FLAKE crumbs, corn, onions, mustard, coriander and remaining ¼ teaspoon pepper sauce. Add crabmeat. Mix well. Shape into four ½-inch thick patties.

3. Place remaining crumbs in shallow dish. Lightly press patties into crumbs, coating both sides.

4. In large nonstick skillet, cook patties in hot butter about 4 minutes or until golden brown, turning once. Serve with mayonnaise mixture.

Caramel Chews

PREP TIME: 20 minutes ■ **TOTAL TIME: 1 hour**

Makes 24 chews (2 per serving)

¼ cup margarine or butter
½ cup granulated sugar
½ cup firmly packed brown sugar
1 egg, slightly beaten
1 cup flaked coconut
5 cups *Kellogg's Corn Flakes®* Cereal

1. Melt margarine in a 3-quart saucepan. Remove from heat and add sugars, stirring until combined. Stir in egg.

2. Add coconut and KELLOGG'S CORN FLAKES cereal, mix lightly. Using level tablespoon, shape into small mounds on baking sheets coated with cooking spray or parchment lined.

3. Bake at 350°F about 10 minutes or until golden brown. Cool completely on pan. Store in airtight container.

Creamy Broccoli-Cauliflower Casserole

PREP TIME: 15 minutes ■ TOTAL TIME: 40 minutes

Makes 8 servings

4 cups broccoli florets
4 cups cauliflowerets
1 medium red bell pepper, chopped
½ cup chopped onion
1 clove garlic, minced
1 tablespoon butter or margarine
1 tablespoon all-purpose flour
1 teaspoon dried basil leaves or Italian seasoning
½ teaspoon lemon pepper seasoning
¼ teaspoon salt
1 cup milk
1 package (8 ounces) reduced-fat cream cheese, softened and cut into pieces
1½ cups *Kellogg's Corn Flakes®* Cereal
2 tablespoons finely shredded Parmesan cheese

1. Cook broccoli, cauliflower and bell pepper in enough boiling salted water to cover for 4 minutes. Drain. Arrange in 12×8×2-inch baking dish coated with cooking spray.

2. In small saucepan, cook onion and garlic in butter until tender. Stir in flour, basil, lemon pepper and salt. Add milk, stirring until smooth. Cook over medium heat until mixture boils, stirring constantly. Continue cooking and stirring 1 minute longer. Remove from heat. Stir in cream cheese until melted. Pour over vegetables in dish.

3. Sprinkle KELLOGG'S CORN FLAKES cereal and Parmesan cheese over vegetables. Bake, uncovered, at 350°F for 25 minutes or until heated through.

MAKE AHEAD: Prepare casserole as above. Cover and refrigerate for 2 to 24 hours. Bake, uncovered, at 350°F about 35 minutes or until heated through.

Creamy Green Bean Casserole

PREP TIME: 20 minutes ■ TOTAL TIME: 40 minutes

Makes 8 servings

- **¼ cup margarine or butter, divided**
- **2 cups *Kellogg's Corn Flakes*® Cereal, crushed to 1½ cups**
- **2 tablespoons flour**
- **¼ teaspoon salt**
- **¼ teaspoon pepper**
- **1 teaspoon sugar**
- **1½ teaspoons onion powder**
- **1 cup low-fat sour cream**
- **1 package (20 ounces) French-style green beans, cooked and drained**
- **1 cup shredded low-fat Swiss cheese (4 ounces)**

1. In 3-quart saucepan, melt margarine over low heat. Remove from heat. Remove 2 tablespoons margarine and mix with KELLOGG'S CORN FLAKES cereal. Set aside for topping.

2. To remaining margarine in pan, stir in flour, salt, pepper, sugar and onion powder. Gradually stir in sour cream. Fold in green beans. Pour into 10×6×2-inch (1½-quart) glass baking dish coated with cooking spray. Sprinkle cheese and cereal mixture over casserole.

3. Bake at 400°F about 20 minutes or until thoroughly heated. Serve hot.

Cherry Bars

PREP TIME: 25 minutes ■ **TOTAL TIME: 1 hour 55 minutes**

Makes 12 bars

- **1 cup all-purpose flour**
- **¼ teaspoon salt**
- **1 teaspoon baking powder**
- **¾ cup firmly packed brown sugar**
- **¼ cup vegetable oil**
- **2 egg whites**
- **1½ cups *Kellogg's Corn Flakes*® Cereal**
- **½ cup chopped maraschino cherries**
- **3 tablespoons maraschino cherries juice**
- **¼ cup chopped almonds**
- **¼ cup powdered sugar**

1. Stir together flour, salt and baking powder. Set aside.

2. In large mixing bowl, combine brown sugar, oil and egg whites. Beat well. Stir in KELLOGG'S CORN FLAKES cereal, cherries and cherry juice. Add flour mixture, stirring until combined. Spread evenly in 8×8×2-inch baking pan coated with cooking spray. Sprinkle with almonds.

3. Bake at 350°F about 30 minutes or until wooden pick inserted near center comes out clean. Cool completely. Dust with powdered sugar before serving. Store tightly covered.